Bitcoin:

The Ultimate Beginner's Guide

Lee Maxwell

© 2016

TABLE OF CONTENT

Introduction

I want to thank you and congratulate you for downloading the book, Bitcoin: The Ultimate Beginner's Guide".

This book contains proven steps and strategies on how to Bitcoin has been in the news the last couple of weeks, but a lot of people are still unaware of them. Could Bitcoin be the future of online currency? This is just one of the questions, frequently asked about Bitcoin.

How Does Bitcoin Work?

Bitcoin is a type of electronic currency (CryptoCurrency) that is autonomous from traditional banking and came into circulation in 2009. According to some of the top online traders, Bitcoin is considered as the best known digital currency that relies on computer networks to solve complex mathematical problems, in order to verify and record the details of each transaction made.

The Bitcoin exchange rate does not depend on the central bank and there is no single authority that governs the supply of CryptoCurrency. However, the Bitcoin price depends on the level of confidence its users have, as the more major companies accept Bitcoin as a method of payment, the more successful Bitcoin will become.

Benefits and Risks of Bitcoin

One of the benefits of Bitcoin is its low inflation risk. Traditional currencies suffer from inflation and they tend to lose their purchasing power each year, as governments continue to use quantative easing to stimulate the economy.

Bitcoin doesn't suffer from low inflation, because Bitcoin mining is limited to just 21 million units. That means the release of new Bitcoins is slowing down and the full amount will be mined out within the next couple of decades. Experts have predicted that the last Bitcoin will be mined by 2050.

.

Thanks again for downloading this book, I hope you enjoy it!

Chapter 1

Introduction to Bitcoin

Bitcoin has been in the news the last couple of weeks, but a lot of people are still unaware of them. Could Bitcoin be the future of online currency? This is just one of the questions, frequently asked about Bitcoin.

How Does Bitcoin Work?

Bitcoin is a type of electronic currency (CryptoCurrency) that is autonomous from traditional banking and came into circulation in 2009. According to some of the top online traders, Bitcoin is considered as the best known digital currency that relies on computer networks to solve complex mathematical problems, in order to verify and record the details of each transaction made.

The Bitcoin exchange rate does not depend on the central bank and there is no single authority that governs the supply of CryptoCurrency. However, the Bitcoin price depends on the level of confidence its users have, as the more major companies accept Bitcoin as a method of payment, the more successful Bitcoin will become.

Benefits and Risks of Bitcoin

One of the benefits of Bitcoin is its low inflation risk. Traditional currencies suffer from inflation and they tend to lose their purchasing power each year, as governments continue to use quantative easing to stimulate the economy.

Bitcoin doesn't suffer from low inflation, because Bitcoin mining is limited to just 21 million units. That means the release of new Bitcoins is slowing down and the full amount will be mined out within the next couple of decades. Experts have predicted that the last Bitcoin will be mined by 2050.

Bitcoin has a low risk of collapse unlike traditional currencies that rely on governments. When currencies collapse, it leads to hyperinflation or the wipeout of one's savings in an instant.

Bitcoin exchange rate is not regulated by any government and is a digital currency available worldwide.

Bitcoin is easy to carry. A billion dollars in the Bitcoin can be stored on a memory stick and placed in one's pocket. It is that easy to transport Bitcoins compared to paper money.

One disadvantage of Bitcoin is its untraceable nature, as Governments and other organisations cannot trace the source of your funds and as such can attract some unscrupulous individuals.

How to Make Money with Bitcoin

Unlike other currencies, there are three ways to make money with Bitcoin, saving, trading and mining. Bitcoin can be traded on open markets, which means you can buy Bitcoin low and sell them high.

Volatility of Bitcoin

The value of Bitcoin dropped in recent weeks because of the abrupt stoppage of trading in Mt. Gox, which is the largest Bitcoin exchange in the world. According to unverified sources, trading was stopped due to malleability-related theft that was said to be worth more than 744,000. The incident has affected the confidence of the investors to the virtual currency.

According to Bitcoin chart, the Bitcoin exchange rate went up to more than $1,100 last December. That was when more people became aware about the digital currency, then the incident with Mt. Gox happened and it dropped to around $530.

In 2014, We expect exponential growth in the popularity of bitcoin around the world with both merchants and consumers, Stephen Pair, BitPay's co-founder and CTO, and anticipate seeing the biggest growth in China, India, Russia and South America.

India has already been cited as the next likely popular market that Bitcoin could move into. Africa could also benefit hugely from using BTC as a currency-of-exchange to get around not having a functioning central bank system or any other country that relies heavily on mobile payments. Bitcoin's expansion in 2014 will be led by Bitcoin ATMs, mobile apps and tools.

World Experiences Bitcoin

More people have accepted the use of Bitcoin and supporters hope that one day, the digital currency will be used by consumers for their online shopping and other electronic deals. Major companies have already accepted payments using the virtual currency. Some of the large firms include Fiverr, TigerDirect and Zynga, among others.

The Future of Bitcoin

Bitcoin works, but critics have said that the digital currency is not ready to be used by the mainstream because of its volatility. They also point to the hacking of the Bitcoin exchange in the past that has resulted in the loss of several millions of dollars.

Supporters of digital currencies have said that there are newer exchanges that are supervised by financial experts and venture capitalists. Experts added that there is still hope for the virtual currency system and the predicted growth is huge.

Chapter 2

How Bitcoin Works

Bitcoins are a decentralized form of crypto currency. Meaning, they are not regulated by a financial institution or the government. As such, unlike a traditional bank account, you do not need a long list a paperwork such as an ID in order for you to establish what's known as a bitcoin wallet. The bitcoin wallet is what you will use to access your bitcoins and to send bitcoins to other individuals.

How To Setup An Account

You can acquire a bitcoin wallet from a bitcoin broker such as Coinbase. When you open up a wallet through a certified broker, you are given a bitcoin address which is a series of numbers and letters, similarly to an account number for a bank account and a private key which is a series of numbers and letters as well, which serve as your password.

How Does Bitcoin Work As An Anonymous Payment Processor

You can do 3 things with bitcoins, you can make a purchase, send money anonymously to someone or utilize it as an investment. More and more merchants have been accepting bitcoins as a form of payment. By utilizing bitcoins instead of cash, you are essentially making that purchase anonymously. The same thing goes for sending money, based on the fact that you do not have to submit a mountain of payment in order for you to establish a bitcoin anonymously, essentially you can send money to someone else anonymously.

How Does Bitcoin Work As An Investment

The price of a bitcoin fluctuates from time to time. Just to put things in perspective, back in the beginning of 2013, the average price of a bitcoin was approximately $400 per bitcoin, but by the end of 2013, the price for bitcoin rose to over $1000. This meant that if you had 2 bitcoins worth $800 in the beginning of 2013 and you stored it as an investment by the end of 2013 those two bitcoins would have been worth over $2000 instead of $800. Many people store bitcoins due to the fact that the value of it fluctuates.

Bitcoin Casino and Poker Sites

Due to the anonymity of bitcoin the gambling industry has taken up bitcoin as a payment method. Both bitcoin casinos and bitcoin poker sites are coming to life and offering their players to make deposits, play with bitcoin at the tables and withdraw directly to their bitcoin wallet. This means that there's no taxes or possibilities for government control. Much like a regular Nevada casino where do you don't need to register anywhere and all your transactions are anonymous.

How Do You Send Bitcoin

In order for you to pay for goods and services or to send bitcoins to an individual, 3 things are needed. Your bitcoin address, your private key and the individual's bitcoin address. From that point, through your bitcoin wallet, you will put 3 pieces of information, which are: input, balance and output. Input refers to your address, balance refers to the amount of bitcoins you are going to send and output is the recipient's address.

How to Buy Bitcoin - Step One

The best way to learn about bitcoin, is to jump in and get a few in your "pocket" to get a feel for how they work.

Despite the hype about how difficult and dangerous it can be, getting bitcoins is a lot easier and safer than you might think. In a lot of ways, it is probably easier than opening an account at a traditional bank.

And, given what has been happening in the banking system, it is probably safer too.

There are a few things to learn: getting and using a software wallet, learning how to send and receive money, learning how to buy bitcoin from a person or an exchange.

Preparation

Before getting started, you will need to get yourself a wallet. You can do this easily enough by registering with one of the exchanges which will host wallet for you. And, although I think you are going to want to have one or more exchange wallets eventually, you should start with one on your own computer both to get a better feel for bitcoin and because the exchanges are still experimental themselves. When we get to that stage of the discussion, I will be advising that you get in the habit of moving your money and coins off the exchanges or diversifying across exchanges to keep your money safe.

What is a wallet?

It is a way to store your bitcoins. Specifically, it is software that has been designed to store bitcoin. It can be run on your desktop computer, laptop, mobile device (except, as yet, Apple) and can also be made to store bitcoins on things like thumb drives. If you are concerned about being hacked, then that is a good option. Even the Winklevoss* twins, who have millions invested in bitcoin, put their investment on hard drives which they then put into a safety deposit box.

*The Winklevoss twins are the ones who originally had the idea for a social networking site that became Facebook. They hired Mark Zuckerberg who took their idea as his own and became immensely rich.

What do you need to know about having a bitcoin wallet on your computer?

Below you can download the original bitcoin wallet, or client, in Windows or Mac format. These are not just wallets, but are in fact part of the bitcoin network. They will receive, store, and send your bitcoins. You can create one or more addresses with a click (an address is a number that looks like this: 1LyFcQatbg4BvT9gGTz6Vd*qq*HKpPn5QB uk). You will see a field where you can copy and paste a number like this from a person you want to send money to and off it will go directly into that person's wallet. You can even create a QR code which will let someone take a picture with an app on their phone and send you some bitcoin. It is perfectly safe to give these out - the address and QR code are both for my donations page. Feel free to donate!

NOTE: This type of wallet acts both as a wallet for you and as part of the bitcoin system. The reason bitcoin works is that every transaction is broadcast and recorded as a number across the entire system (meaning that every transaction is confirmed and made irreversible by the network itself). Any computer with the right software can be part of that system, checking and supporting the network. This wallet serves as your personal wallet and also as a support for that system. Therefore, be aware that it will take up 8-9 gigabytes of your computer's memory. After you install the wallet, it will take as much as a day for the wallet to sync with the network. This is normal, does not harm your computer, and makes the system as a whole more secure, so it's a good idea.

Bitcoin Qt

The original wallet.

This is a full-featured wallet: create multiple addresses to receive bitcoins, send bitcoins easily, track transactions, and back up your wallet.

Outside of the time it takes to sync, this is a very easy to use option.

Search for Bitcoin Qt wallet download to find their site.

Armory

Runs on top of Bitcoi Qt, so it has all of the same syncing requirements.

Armory allows you to back up, encrypt, and the ability to store your bitcoins off line.

Search for Bitcoin Armory Wallet to find their site.

If you don't want to have that much memory used or don't want to wait for your wallet to sync, there are good wallets that do not make you sync the entire history of bitcocin:

Multibit

A lightweight wallet that syncs *q*uickly. This is very good for new users.

Search for Bitcoin Multibit Wallet to find their site.

Electum

In addition to being quick and light, this wallet allows you to recover lost data using a passcode.

Search for Bitcoin Electum Wallet to find their site.

After you get the wallet set up, take a few minutes clicking around. Things to look for:

o There will be a page that shows you how many bitcoins are currently in your wallet. Keep in mind that bitcoins can be broken up into smaller pieces, so you may see a decimal with a lot of zeros after it. (Interesting note, 0.00000001 is one Satoshi, named after the pseudonymous creator of bitcoin).

o There will be an area showing what your recent transactions are.

o There will be an area where you can create an address and a QR code (like the one I have above). You don't need the QR code if you don't want it, but if you run a business and you want to accept bitcoin, then all you'll need to do to accept payment is to show someone the QR code, let them take a picture of it, and they will be able to send you some money. You will also be able to create as many addresses as you like, so if you want to track where the money is coming from, you could have a separately labeled address from each one of your payees.

o There will be an area with a box for you to paste a code when you want to send money to someone or to yourself on an exchange or different wallet.

There will be other options and features, but to start out with, these are the items that you should know about.

Chapter 3

Getting Your First Bitcoins

Now that you have a wallet, you will, of course, want to test them out.

The very first place to go is faucet.bitcoin....

This is a website that gives out small amounts of bitcoin for the purpose of getting people used to using them. The original version of this was run by the lead developer of bitcoin, Gavin Andreson. That site has since closed and this site operates by sending out one or two advertisements a month. You agree to receive those messages by requesting the bitcoins. Copy and paste your new bitcoin address and enter a phone number to which you can receive an SMS. They send out an SMS to be sure that people are not continuously coming back for more since it costs nothing to create a bitcoin address. They will also send out once or twice a month advertisement to support their operation. The amount they send it trivial: 0.0015 BTC (or 1.5 mBTC). However, they process almost immediately and you can check to see that your address and wallet are working. It is also *q*uite a feeling to get that portion of a bitcoin. (Non-disclaimer: I have no connection with this site and receive nothing if you use them. I simply think they are a good way to get your feet wet).

Congratulations! You have just entered the bitcoin economy.

To get your feet a little wetter, you can go panning for gold. There are a number of services and websites out there that will pay you in bitcoin to do things like go to certain websites, fill out online surveys, or watch sponsored videos. These are harmless, and you can earn a few extra bitcoins this way, but it is important to remember that these are businesses that get paid when people click on the links on their sites. They are essentially kicking back a portion of what they get paid to you. There is nothing illegal, or even immoral about this (you might like what you see and make a purchase!), but they are frequently flashy and may not be completely straightforward. All the ones that I have tried (particularly bitvisitor.com) have paid out as advertised. It is interesting to experiment with these, but even with the likely rise in the value of bitcoin, you won't become a millionaire doing this. So, unless you are an advertisement junkie, I would recommend you move on. If you would like to try, simply Google "free bitcoins" or something along those lines and you will find numerous sites.

Buying Bitcoin Hand-to-Hand

Finally, this is going to be the real test of bitcoin. Can people easily trade them back and forth? If this can't happen, then there can't really be a bitcoin economy because retailers won't be able to use it. If retailers can't use it, what earthly good is it? Fortunately, this is not really a problem. iPhone is a bit of a hold out, but many smartphones have apps (mobile wallets) that will read QR codes and allow you to send bitcoin to whomever you want. You can also display a QR code of your address, or even carry a card in your wallet with your QR code to let people send bitcoin to you. Depending on what kind of wallet you have, you can then check to see if the bitcoins have been received.

A couple of things to note:

When you set up your wallet, if you click around a bit, you will see an option to pay a fee to speed transactions. This money becomes available to a bitcoin miner as he/she/they process bitcoin information. The miners doing the work of creating blocks of information keeps the system up to date and secure. The fee is an incentive to the miner to be sure to include your information in the next information block and therefore "verify" it. In the short term, miners are making most of their money by mining new coins (check the section on What Are Bitcoins for more information about this). In the long term, as it gets harder to find new coins, and as the economy increases, the fees will be an incentive for miners to keep creating more blocks and keep the economy going. Your wallet should be set to pay 0 fees as a default, but if you want, you can add a fee to prioritize your transactions. You are under no obligation to pay a fee, and many organizations that process many small transactions (like the ones that pan for gold described above) produce enough fees to keep the miners happy.

In clicking around your wallet, on the transactions page or linked to specific transactions, you will see a note about confirmations. When you make a transaction, that information is sent out into the network and the network will send back a confirmation that there is no double entry for that bitcoin. It is smart to wait until you get several confirmations before walking away from someone who has paid you. It is actually not very easy to scam someone hand-to-hand like this, and it is not very cost-effective for the criminal, but it can be done.

Where can you buy bitcoin like this?

You may have a bitcoin Meetup in your area.

You can check out localbitcoins.com to find people near you who are interested in buying or selling.

Some are trying to start up local street exchanges across the world. These are called Buttonwoods after the first street exchange established on Wall Street in 1792 under a buttonwood tree. See if there is one, or start one, in your area.

See if you have any friends who would like to try bitcoins out. Actually, the more people who start using bitcoin, the larger and more successful it will be come. So please tell two friends!

Some people ask if it is possible to buy physical bitcoins. The answer to this is both a yes and a no. Bitcoin, by its very nature, is a digital currency and has no physical form. However, there are a couple of ways that you can practically hold a bitcoin in your hands:

Cascascius Coins: These are the brainchild of Mike Caldwell. He mints physical coins and then embeds the private keys for the bitcoins inside them. You can get the private key by peeling a hologram from the coin which will then clearly show that the coin has been tampered with. Mike has gone out of his way to ensure that he can be trusted. These are a good investment strategy as in the years to come it may be that these coins are huge collector's items.

Paper Wallets: A paper wallet just means that rather than keeping the information for your bitcoin stored in a digital wallet, you print the key information off along with a private key and keep it safe in a safe, in a drawer, or in your mattress (if you like). This is highly recommended and cost effective system for keeping your bitcoin safe. Keep in mind, though, that someone could steal them or if your house burns, they will go with the house and there will be no way to get them back. Really, no different than cash. Also, as with Casascius Coins, they will not really be good for spending until you put them back into the computer.

* There is software to make printing your paper wallets easier. bitcoinpaperwallet.com is one of the best and includes a good tutorial about how to use them.

* The bitcoins are not actually in the wallet, they are still on the web. In fact, the outside of the wallet will have a QR code that will allow you ship coins to the wallet any time you like.

* The sealed part of the wallet will have the private key without which you cannot access the coins. Therefore, only put as many coins on the wallet as you want to be inaccessible. You will not be able to whip this thing out and take out a few coins to buy a cup of coffee. Rather, think of it as a piggy bank. To get the money, you have to smash it. It is possible to take out smaller amounts, but at this point the security of the wallet is compromised and it would be easier for someone to steal the coins. Better to have them all in or out.

* People who use paper wallets are usually security conscious, and there are a number of ways for the nefarious in the world to hack your computer. Bitcoinpaperwallet.com gives a lot of good advice about how to print your wallets securely.

Some people have also asked about buying bitcoins on eBay. Yes, it is possible, but they will be far overpriced. So, selling on eBay might seem to be a better option given the extreme markup over market value you might see. But, as with anything that is too good to be true, this is too good to be true. As I will explain in the next section, selling bitcoin this way is just way too risky.

How Not to Buy Bitcoin

In the next section, I am going to explain a couple of key points about buying from Bitcoin Exchanges. Before I do, let me give you a warning.

A short history lesson: When people first started setting up actual business based on bitcoin, they used all of the tools available to any merchant. They sold by credit card and PayPal. The problem with this business model was quickly spotted: bitcoin transactions are not reversible by anyone except the recipient of the money. Credit cards and PayPal have strong buyer protection policies that make it relatively easy for people to request a chargeback. So, nefarious individuals realized this and began making purchases of bitcoin and then sooner or later requesting a chargeback. And, since bitcoin is a non-physical product, sent by new and poorly understood technological means, the sellers were not able to contest this. Because of this, sellers stopped accepting credit cards and PayPal.

This was a big problem for the currency: How to move money between buyers and seller? Some business emerged that would credit you with bitcoin if you wired them money. Very often these businesses would give addresses in Albania, Poland, or Russia. The fact is that many of these did work and there are a lot of stories on the forums of people who bought bitcoins this way. But it took a lot of time and in the meantime the buyer just had to bite his or her fingernails wondering if they would get their bitcoins or kiss their investment goodbye.

I expect that as bitcoin becomes more acceptable and valuable, we are going to see a version of the Nigerian Prince scam. So the warning is this: we now have exchanges and other businesses that allow for moving money easily onto and off of exchanges. Never wire money for bitcoin. It was a short-lived, and well-forgotten, moment in the history of bitcoin.

Bitcoin: What Is It, and Is It Right for Your Business?

OK, so what's Bitcoin?

It's not an actual coin, it's "cryptocurrency," a digital form of payment that is produced ("mined") by lots of people worldwide. It allows peer-to-peer transactions instantly, worldwide, for free or at very low cost.

Bitcoin was invented after decades of research into cryptography by software developer, Satoshi Nakamoto (believed to be a pseudonym), who designed the algorithm and introduced it in 2009. His true identity remains a mystery.

This currency is not backed by a tangible commodity (such as gold or silver); bitcoins are traded online which makes them a commodity in themselves.

Bitcoin is an open-source product, accessible by anyone who is a user. All you need is an email address, Internet access, and money to get started.

Chapter 4

Where does it come from?

Bitcoin is mined on a distributed computer network of users running specialized software; the network solves certain mathematical proofs, and searches for a particular data sequence ("block") that produces a particular pattern when the BTC algorithm is applied to it. A match produces a bitcoin. It's complex and time- and energy-consuming.

Only 21 million bitcoins are ever to be mined (about 11 million are currently in circulation). The math problems the network computers solve get progressively more difficult to keep the mining operations and supply in check.

This network also validates all the transactions through cryptography.

How does Bitcoin work?

Internet users transfer digital assets (bits) to each other on a network. There is no online bank; rather, Bitcoin has been described as an Internet-wide distributed ledger. Users buy Bitcoin with cash or by selling a product or service for Bitcoin. Bitcoin wallets store and use this digital currency. Users may sell out of this virtual ledger by trading their Bitcoin to someone else who wants in. Anyone can do this, anywhere in the world.

There are smartphone apps for conducting mobile Bitcoin transactions and Bitcoin exchanges are populating the Internet.

How is Bitcoin valued?

Bitcoin is not held or controlled by a financial institution; it is completely decentralized. Unlike real-world money it cannot be devalued by governments or banks.

Instead, Bitcoin's value lies simply in its acceptance between users as a form of payment and because its supply is finite. Its global currency values fluctuate according to supply and demand and market speculation; as more people create wallets and hold and spend bitcoins, and more businesses accept it, Bitcoin's value will rise. Banks are now trying to value Bitcoin and some investment websites predict the price of a bitcoin will be several thousand dollars in 2014.

What are its benefits?

There are benefits to consumers and merchants that want to use this payment option.

1. Fast transactions - Bitcoin is transferred instantly over the Internet.

2. No fees/low fees -- Unlike credit cards, Bitcoin can be used for free or very low fees. Without the centralized institution as middle man, there are no authorizations (and fees) required. This improves profit margins sales.

3. Eliminates fraud risk -Only the Bitcoin owner can send payment to the intended recipient, who is the only one who can receive it. The network knows the transfer has occurred and transactions are validated; they cannot be challenged or taken back. This is big for online merchants who are often subject to credit card processors' assessments of whether or not a transaction is fraudulent, or businesses that pay the high price of credit card chargebacks.

4. Data is secure -- As we have seen with recent hacks on national retailers' payment processing systems, the Internet is not always a secure place for private data. With Bitcoin, users do not give up private information.

a. They have two keys - a public key that serves as the bitcoin address and a private key with personal data.

b. Transactions are "signed" digitally by combining the public and private keys; a mathematical function is applied and a certificate is generated proving the user initiated the transaction. Digital signatures are unique to each transaction and cannot be re-used.

c. The merchant/recipient never sees your secret information (name, number, physical address) so it's somewhat anonymous but it is traceable (to the bitcoin address on the public key).

5. Convenient payment system -- Merchants can use Bitcoin entirely as a payment system; they do not have to hold any Bitcoin currency since Bitcoin can be converted to dollars. Consumers or merchants can trade in and out of Bitcoin and other currencies at any time.

6. International payments - Bitcoin is used around the world; e-commerce merchants and service providers can easily accept international payments, which open up new potential marketplaces for them.

7. Easy to track -- The network tracks and permanently logs every transaction in the Bitcoin block chain (the database). In the case of possible wrongdoing, it is easier for law enforcement officials to trace these transactions.

8. Micropayments are possible - Bitcoins can be divided down to one one-hundred-millionth, so running small payments of a dollar or less becomes a free or near-free transaction. This could be a real boon for convenience stores, coffee shops, and subscription-based websites (videos, publications).

Still a little confused? Here are a few examples of transactions:

Bitcoin in the retail environment

At checkout, the payer uses a smartphone app to scan a QR code with all the transaction information needed to transfer the bitcoin to the retailer. Tapping the "Confirm" button completes the transaction. If the user doesn't own any Bitcoin, the network converts dollars in his account into the digital currency.

The retailer can convert that Bitcoin into dollars if it wants to, there were no or very low processing fees (instead of 2 to 3 percent), no hackers can steal personal consumer information, and there is no risk of fraud. Very slick.

Bitcoins in hospitality

Hotels can accept Bitcoin for room and dining payments on the premises for guests who wish to pay by Bitcoin using their mobile wallets, or PC-to-website to pay for a reservation online. A third-party

BTC merchant processor can assist in handling the transactions which it clears over the Bitcoin network. These processing clients are installed on tablets at the establishments' front desk or in the restaurants for users with BTC smartphone apps. (These payment processors are also available for desktops, in retail POS systems, and integrated into foodservice POS systems.) No credit cards or money need to change hands.

These cashless transactions are fast and the processor can convert bitcoins into currency and make a daily direct deposit into the establishment's bank account. It was announced in January 2014 that two Las Vegas hotel-casinos will accept Bitcoin payments at the front desk, in their restaurants, and in the gift shop.

It sounds good - so what's the catch?

Business owners should consider issues of participation, security and cost.

• A relatively small number of ordinary consumers and merchants currently use or understand Bitcoin. However, adoption is increasing globally and tools and technologies are being developed to make participation easier.

• It's the Internet, so hackers are threats to the exchanges. The Economist reported that a Bitcoin exchange was hacked in September 2013 and $250,000 in bitcoins was stolen from users' online vaults. Bitcoins can be stolen like other currency, so vigilant network, server and database security is paramount.

• Users must carefully safeguard their bitcoin wallets which contain their private keys. Secure backups or printouts are crucial.

• Bitcoin is not regulated or insured by the US government so there is no insurance for your account if the exchange goes out of business or is robbed by hackers.

- Bitcoins are relatively expensive. Current rates and selling prices are available on the online exchanges.

The virtual currency is not yet universal but it is gaining market awareness and acceptance. A business may decide to try Bitcoin to save on credit card and bank fees, as a customer convenience, or to see if it helps or hinders sales and profitability.

In Bitcoin We Trust?

By now you have probably heard of Bitcoin, but can you define it?

Most often it is described as a non-government digital currency. Bitcoin is also sometimes called a cybercurrency or, in a nod to its encrypted origins, a cryptocurrency. Those descriptions are accurate enough, but they miss the point.

It's like describing the U.S. dollar as a green piece of paper with pictures on it.

I have my own ways of describing Bitcoin. I think of it as store credit without the store. A prepaid phone without the phone. Precious metal without the metal. Legal tender for no debts, public or private, unless the party to whom it is tendered wishes to accept it. An instrument backed by the full faith and credit only of its anonymous creators, in whom I therefore place no faith, and to whom I give no credit except for ingenuity.

I wouldn't touch a bitcoin with a 10-foot USB cable. But a fair number of people already have, and quite a few more soon may.

This is partly because entrepreneurs Cameron and Tyler Winklevoss, best known for their role in the origins of Facebook, are now seeking to use their technological savvy, and money, to bring Bitcoin into the mainstream.

The Winklevosses hope to start an exchange-traded fund for bitcoins. An ETF would make Bitcoin more widely available to investors who lack the technological know-how to purchase the digital currency directly. As of April, the Winklevosses are said to have held around 1 percent of all existent bitcoins.

Created in 2009 by an anonymous cryptographer, Bitcoin operates on the premise that anything, even intangible bits of code, can have value so long as enough people decide to treat it as valuable. Bitcoins exist only as digital representations and are not pegged to any traditional currency.

According to the Bitcoin website, "Bitcoin is designed around the idea of a new form of money that uses cryptography to control its creation and transactions, rather than relying on central authorities." (1) New bitcoins are "mined" by users who solve computer algorithms to discover virtual coins. Bitcoins' purported creators have said that the ultimate supply of bitcoins will be capped at 21 million.

While Bitcoin promotes itself as "a very secure and inexpensive way to handle payments," (2) in reality few businesses have made the move to accept bitcoins. Of those that have, a sizable number operate in the black market.

Bitcoins are traded anonymously over the Internet, without any participation on the part of established financial institutions. As of 2012, sales of drugs and other black-market goods accounted for an estimated 20 percent of exchanges from bitcoins to U.S. dollars on the main Bitcoin exchange, called Mt. Gox. The Drug Enforcement Agency recently conducted its first-ever Bitcoin seizure, after reportedly tying a transaction on the anonymous Bitcoin-only marketplace Silk Road to the sale of prescription and illegal drugs.

Some Bitcoin users have also suggested that the currency can serve as a means to avoid taxes. That may be true, but only in the sense that bitcoins aid illegal tax evasion, not in the sense that they actually serve any role in genuine tax planning. Under federal tax law, no cash needs to change hands in order for a taxable transaction to occur. Barter and other non-cash exchanges are still fully taxable. There is no reason that transactions involving bitcoins would be treated differently.

Outside of the criminal element, Bitcoin's main devotees are speculators, who have no intention of using bitcoins to buy anything. These investors are convinced that the limited supply of bitcoins will force their value to follow a continual upward trajectory.

Bitcoin has indeed seen some significant spikes in value. But it has also experienced major losses, including an 80 percent decline over 24 hours in April. At the start of this month, bitcoins were down to around $90, from a high of $266 before the April crash. They were trading near $97 earlier this week, according to mtgox.com.

The Winklevosses would make Bitcoin investing easier by allowing smaller-scale investors to profit, or lose, as the case may be, without the hassle of actually buying and storing the electronic coins. Despite claims of security, Bitcoin storage has proved problematic. In 2011, an attack on the Mt. Gox exchange forced it to temporarily shut down and caused the price of bitcoins to briefly fall to nearly zero. Since Bitcoin transactions are all anonymous, there is little chance of tracking down the culprits if you suddenly find your electronic wallet empty. If the Winklevosses get regulatory approval, their ETF would help shield investors from the threat of individual theft. The ETF, however, would do nothing to address the problem of volatility caused by large-scale thefts elsewhere in the Bitcoin market.

While Bitcoin comes wrapped in a high-tech veneer, this newest of currencies has a surprising amount in common with one of the oldest currencies: gold. Bitcoin's own vocabulary, particularly the term "mining," highlights this connection, and intentionally so. The mining process is designed to be difficult as a control on supply, mimicking the extraction of more conventional resources from the ground. Far from providing a sense of security, however, this rhetoric ought to serve as a word of caution.

Gold is an investment of last resort. It has little intrinsic value. It does not generate interest. But because its supply is finite, it is seen as being more stable than forms of money that can be printed at will.

The problem with gold is that it doesn't do anything. Since gold coins have fallen out of use, most of the world's gold now sits in the vaults of central banks and other financial institutions. As a result, gold has little connection to the real economy. That can seem like a good thing when the real economy feels like a scary place to be. But as soon as other attractive investment options appear, gold loses its shine. That is what we have seen with the recent declines in gold prices.

In their push to bring Bitcoin to the mainstream, its promoters have accepted, and, in some cases sought out, increased regulation. Last month Mt. Gox registered itself as a money services business with the Treasury Department's Financial Crimes Enforcement Network. It has also increased customer verification measures. The changes came in response to a March directive from Financial Crimes Enforcement Network clarifying the application of its rules to virtual currencies. The Winklevosses' proposed ETF would bring a new level of accountability.

In the end, however, I expect that Bitcoin will fade back into the shadows of the black market. Those who want a regulated, secure currency that they can use for legitimate business transactions will pick from one of the many currencies already sponsored by a national government equipped with ample resources, a real-world economy and far more transparency and security than the Bitcoin world can offer.

After the Bitcoin bubble bursts, we won't even be able to use the leftover coins for jewelry.

Chapter 5

5 Merits of Bitcoins That You Didn't Know

Most people have heard of the term Bitcoin but don't have a clear idea of what it really is. Simply defined, Bitcoin is a decentralized, peer to peer, digital currency system, designed to give online users the ability to process transactions via digital unit of exchange known as Bitcoins. In other words, it is a virtual currency.

The Bitcoin system was created in the year 2009 by an undisclosed programmer(s). Since then, Bitcoin has garnered huge attention as well as controversy as an alternative to US dollar, Euros and commodity currencies such as gold and silver.

A private network of computers connected by a shared program is used to carry out transactions and process payments in Bitcoin. The creation of Bitcoins are based on increasingly complex mathematical algorithms and its purchase is made with standard national money currencies. Users of Bitcoin can access their coins with their smart phones or computers.

As a new and growing virtual currency, Bitcoin has certain distinct advantages over the conventional government flat currencies. Here are 5 benefits that you will enjoy when using Bitcoin

1) No Taxation

When you make purchases via dollars, euros or any other government flat currency, you have to pay an addition sum of money to the government as tax. Every purchasable item has its own designated tax rate. However, when you're making a purchase through Bitcoin, sales taxes are not added to your purchase. This is deemed as a legal form of tax evasion and is one of the major advantages of being a Bitcoin user.

With zero tax rates, Bitcoin can come in handy especially when purchasing luxury items that are exclusive to a foreign land. Such items, more often than not, are heavily taxed by the government.

2) Flexible Online Payments

Bitcoin is an online payment system and just like any other such system, the users of Bitcoin have the luxury of paying for their coins from any corner of the world that has an internet connection. This means that you could be lying on your bed and purchasing coins instead of taking the pain of travelling to a specific bank or store to get your work done.

Moreover, an online payment via Bitcoin does not require you to fill in details about your personal information. Hence, Bitcoin processing Bitcoin transactions is a lot simpler than those carried out through U.S. Bank accounts and credit cards.

3) Minimal Transaction Fees

Fees and exchange costs are a part and parcel of standard wire transfers and international purchases. Bitcoin is not monitored or moderated by any intermediary institution or government agency. Therefore, the costs of transacting are kept very low unlike international transactions made via conventional currencies.

In addition to this, transactions in Bitcoin are not known to be time consuming since it does not involve the complications of typical authorization requirements and waiting periods.

4) Concealed User Identity

All Bitcoin transactions are discrete, or in other words Bitcoin gives you the option of User anonymity. Bitcoins are similar to cash only purchases in the sense that your transactions can never be tracked back to you and these purchases are never connected with your personal identity. As a matter of fact, the Bitcoin address that is created for user purchases is never the same for two different transactions.

If you want to, you do have the option of voluntarily revealing and publishing your Bitcoin transactions but in most cases users keep their identities secret.

5) No outside interventions

One of the greatest advantages of Bitcoin is that it eliminates third party interruptions. This means that governments, banks and other financial intermediaries have no authority whatsoever to disrupt user transactions or freeze a Bitcoin account. As mentioned before, Bitcoin is based strictly on a peer to peer system. Hence, the users of Bitcoin enjoy greater liberty when making purchases with Bitcoins than they do when using conventional national currencies.

Digital currencies such as the Bitcoin are comparatively new and haven't yet been put through major tests. As a result, many feel that there are certain risks involved in the usage of Bitcoin. Regardless of the potential disadvantages of Bitcoin, it's evident that its merits are strong enough to make it a legitimate contender to challenge conventional currencies in the not so distant future.

The IRS Takes A Position On Bitcoin

Bitcoin used to be something like Schrodinger's currency. Without regulatory observers, it could claim to be money and property at the same time.

Now the Internal Revenue Service has opened the box, and the virtual currency's condition is established - at least for federal tax purposes.

The IRS recently issued guidance on how it will treat bitcoin, and any other stateless electronic competitor. The short answer: as property, not currency. Bitcoin, along with other virtual currencies that can be exchanged for legal tender, will now be treated in most cases as a capital asset, and in a few situations as inventory. Bitcoin holders who are not dealers will be subject to capital gains tax on increases in value. Bitcoin "miners," who unlock the currency's algorithms, will need to report their finds as income, just as other miners do when extracting more traditional resources.

Though this decision is unlikely to cause much turbulence, it is worth noting. Now that the IRS has made a call, investors and bitcoin enthusiasts can move forward with a more accurate understanding of what they are (virtually) holding. A bitcoin holder who wants to comply with the tax law, rather than evade it, now knows how to do so.

I think the IRS is correct in determining that bitcoin is not money. Bitcoin, and other virtual currencies like it, is too unstable in value for it to realistically be called a form of currency. In this era of floating exchange rates, it's true that the value of nearly all currencies changes from week to week or year to year relative to any particular benchmark, whether it's the dollar or a barrel of oil. But a key feature of money is to serve as a store of value. The worth of the money itself should not change drastically from day to day or hour to hour.

Bitcoin utterly fails this test. Buying a bitcoin is a speculative investment. It is not a place to park your idle, spendable cash. Further, to my knowledge, no mainstream financial institution will pay interest on bitcoin deposits in the form of more bitcoins. Any return on a bitcoin holding comes solely from a change in the bitcoin's value.

Whether the IRS' decision will help or hurt current bitcoin holders depends on why they wanted bitcoins in the first place. For those hoping to profit directly from bitcoin's fluctuations in value, this is good news, as the rules for capital gains and losses are relatively favorable to taxpayers. This characterization also upholds the way some high-profile bitcoin enthusiasts, including the Winklevoss twins, have reported their earnings in the absence of clear guidance. (While the new treatment of bitcoin is applicable to past years, penalty relief may be available to taxpayers who can demonstrate reasonable cause for their positions.)

For those hoping to use bitcoin to pay their rent or buy coffee, the decision adds complexity, since spending bitcoin is treated as a taxable form of barter. Those who spend bitcoins, and those who accept them as payment, will both need to note the fair market value of the bitcoin on the date the transaction occurs. This will be used to calculate the spender's capital gains or losses and the receiver's basis for future gains or losses.

While the triggering event - the transaction - is easy to identify, determining a particular bitcoin's basis, or its holding period in order to determine whether short-term or long-term capital gains tax rates apply, may prove challenging. For an investor, that might be an acceptable hassle. But when you are deciding whether to buy your latte with a bitcoin or just pull five dollars out of your wallet, the simplicity of the latter is likely to win the day. The IRS guidance simply makes clear what was already true: Bitcoin isn't a new form of cash. Its benefits and drawbacks are different.

The IRS has also clarified several other points. If an employer pays a worker in virtual currency, that payment counts as wages for employment tax purposes. And if businesses make payments worth $600 or more to independent contractors using bitcoin, the businesses will be required to file Forms 1099, just as they would if they paid the contractors in cash.

Clearer rules may cause new administrative headaches for some bitcoin users, but they could ensure bitcoin's future at a time when investors have good reason to be wary. "[Bitcoin is] getting legitimacy, which it didn't have previously," Ajay Vinze, the associate dean at Arizona State University's business school, told The New York Times. He said the IRS decision "puts Bitcoin on a track to becoming a true financial asset." (1)

Once all bitcoin users can recognize and agree on the type of asset it is, that outcome is likelier.

A minority of bitcoin users saw its former unregulated status as a feature, not a drawback. Some of them oppose government oversight for ideological reasons, while others found bitcoin a useful way to conduct illicit business. But as the recent collapse of prominent bitcoin exchange Mt. Gox demonstrated, unregulated bitcoin exchange can lead to catastrophic losses with no safety net. Some users may have thought they were protecting themselves by fleeing to bitcoin to escape the heavily regulated banking industry, but no regulation at all isn't the answer either.

The IRS is correct when it says that bitcoin should be treated as property. This certainty may secure the future of an asset that, while it makes poor currency, might be useful to those who want to hold it as property for speculative or commercial reasons.

What Is Bitcoin and Is It a Good Investment?

Bitcoin (BTC) is a new kind of digital currency-with cryptographic keys-that is decentralized to a network of computers used by users and miners around the world and is not controlled by a single organization or government. It is the first digital cryptocurrency that has gained the public's attention and is accepted by a growing number of merchants. Like other currencies, users can use the digital currency to buy goods and services online as well as in some physical stores that accept it as a form of payment. Currency traders can also trade Bitcoins in Bitcoin exchanges.

There are several major differences between Bitcoin and traditional currencies (e.g. U.S. dollar):

Bitcoin does not have a centralized authority or clearing house (e.g. government, central bank, MasterCard or Visa network). The peer-to-peer payment network is managed by users and miners around the world. The currency is anonymously transferred directly between users through the internet without going through a clearing house. This means that transaction fees are much lower.

Bitcoin is created through a process called "Bitcoin mining". Miners around the world use mining software and computers to solve complex bitcoin algorithms and to approve Bitcoin transactions. They are awarded with transaction fees and new Bitcoins generated from solving Bitcoin algorithms.

There is a limited amount of Bitcoins in circulation. According to Blockchain, there were about 12.1 million in circulation as of Dec. 20, 2013. The difficulty to mine Bitcoins (solve algorithms) becomes harder as more Bitcoins are generated, and the maximum amount in circulation is capped at 21 million. The limit will not be reached until approximately the year 2140. This makes Bitcoins more valuable as more people use them.

A public ledger called 'Blockchain' records all Bitcoin transactions and shows each Bitcoin owner's respective holdings. Anyone can access the public ledger to verify transactions. This makes the digital currency more transparent and predictable. More importantly, the transparency prevents fraud and double spending of the same Bitcoins.

The digital currency can be acquired through Bitcoin mining or Bitcoin exchanges.

The digital currency is accepted by a limited number of merchants on the web and in some brick-and-mortar retailers.

Bitcoin wallets (similar to PayPal accounts) are used for storing Bitcoins, private keys and public addresses as well as for anonymously transferring Bitcoins between users.

Bitcoins are not insured and are not protected by government agencies. Hence, they cannot be recovered if the secret keys are stolen by a hacker or lost to a failed hard drive, or due to the closure of a Bitcoin exchange. If the secret keys are lost, the associated Bitcoins cannot be recovered and would be out of circulation. Visit this link for an FAQ on Bitcoins.

I believe that Bitcoin will gain more acceptance from the public because users can remain anonymous while buying goods and services online, transactions fees are much lower than credit card payment networks; the public ledger is accessible by anyone, which can be used to prevent fraud; the currency supply is capped at 21 million, and the payment network is operated by users and miners instead of a central authority.

However, I do not think that it is a great investment vehicle because it is extremely volatile and is not very stable. For example, the bitcoin price grew from around $14 to a peak of $1,200 USD this year before dropping to $632 per BTC at the time of writing.

Bitcoin surged this year because investors speculated that the currency would gain wider acceptance and that it would increase in price. The currency plunged 50% in December because BTC China (China's largest Bitcoin operator) announced that it could no longer accept new deposits due to government regulations. And according to Bloomberg, the Chinese central bank barred financial institutions and payment companies from handling bitcoin transactions.

Bitcoin will likely gain more public acceptance over time, but its price is extremely volatile and very sensitive to news-such as government regulations and restrictions-that could negatively impact the currency.

Therefore, I do not suggest investors to invest in Bitcoins unless they were purchased at a less than $10 USD per BTC because this would allow for a much larger margin of safety.

Otherwise, I believe that it is much better to invest in stocks that have strong fundamentals, as well as great business prospects and management teams because the underlying companies have intrinsic values and are more predictable.

Bitcoin Vs Goldcoin

Bitcoin... Monetary Nirvana?

If you don't know what Bitcoin is, do a bit of research on the internet, and you will get plenty... but the short story is that Bitcoin was created as a medium of exchange, without a central bank or bank of issue being involved. Furthermore, Bitcoin transactions are supposed to be private, that is anonymous. Most interestingly, Bitcoins have no real world existence; they exist only in computer software, as a kind of virtual reality.

The general idea is that Bitcoins are 'mined'... interesting term here... by solving an increasingly difficult mathematical formula -more difficult as more Bitcoins are 'mined' into existence; again interesting- on a computer. Once created, the new Bitcoin is put into an electronic 'wallet'. It is then possible to trade real goods or Fiat currency for Bitcoins... and vice versa. Furthermore, as there is no central issuer of Bitcoins, it is all highly distributed, thus resistant to being 'managed' by authority.

Naturally proponents of Bitcoin, those who benefit from the growth of Bitcoin, insist rather loudly that 'for sure, Bitcoin is money'... and not only that, but 'it is the best money ever, the money of the future', etc... Well, the proponents of Fiat shout just as loudly that paper currency is money... and we all know that Fiat paper is not money by any means, as it lacks the most important attributes of real money. The question then is does Bitcoin even qualify as money... never mind it being the money of the future, or the best money ever.

To find out, let's look at the attributes that define money, and see if Bitcoin qualifies. The three essential attributes of money are;

1) money is a stable store of value; the most essential attribute, as without stability of value the function of numeraire, or unit of measure of value, fails.

2) money is the numeraire, the unit of account.

3) money is a medium of exchange... but other things can also fulfill this function ie direct barter, the 'netting out' of goods exchanged. Also 'trade goods' (chits) that hold value temporarily; and finally exchange of mutual credit; ie netting out the value of promises fulfilled by exchanging bills or IOU's.

Compared to Fiat, Bitcoin does not do too badly as a medium of exchange. Fiat is only accepted in the geographic domain of its issuer. Dollars are no good in

Europe etc. Bitcoin is accepted internationally. On the other hand, very few retailers currently accept payment in Bitcoin. Unless the acceptance grows geometrically, Fiat wins... although at the cost of exchange between countries.

The first condition is a lot tougher; money must be a stable store of value... now Bitcoins have gone from a 'value' of $3.00 to around $1,000, in just a few years. This is about as far from being a 'stable store of value'; as you can get! Indeed, such gains are a perfect example of a speculative boom... like Dutch tulip bulbs, or junior mining companies, or Nortel stocks.

Of course, Fiat fails here as well; for example, the US Dollar, the 'main' Fiat, has lost over 95% of its value in a few decades... neither fiat nor Bitcoin qualify in the most important measure of money; the capacity to store value and preserve value through time. Real money, that is Gold, has shown the ability to hold value not just for centuries, but for eons.

Neither Fiat nor Bitcoin has this crucial capacity... both fail as money.

Finally, we come to the second attribute; that of being the numeraire. Now this is really interesting, and we can see why both Bitcoin and Fiat fail as money, by looking closely at the question of the 'numeraire'. Numeraire refers to the use of money to not only store value, but to in a sense measure, or compare value. In Austrian economics, it is considered impossible to actually measure value; after all, value resides only in human consciousness... and how can anything in consciousness actually be measured? Nevertheless, through the principle of Mengerian market action, that is interaction between bid and offer, market prices can be established... if only momentarily... and this market price is expressed in terms of the numeraire, the most marketable good, that is money.

So how do we establish the value of Fiat... ? Through the concept of 'purchasing power'... that is, the value of Fiat is determined by what it can be traded for...

a so called 'basket of goods'. But his clearly implies that Fiat has no value of its own, rather value flows from the value of the goods and services it may be traded for. Causality flows from the goods 'bought' to the Fiat number. After all, what difference is there between a one Dollar bill and a hundred Dollar bill, except the number printed on it... and the purchasing power of the number?

Gold, on the other hand, is not measured by what it trades for; rather, uniquely, it is measured by another physical standard; by its weight, or mass. A gram of Gold is a gram of gold, and an ounce of Gold is an ounce of Gold... no matter what number is engraved on its surface, 'face value' or otherwise. Causality is the opposite to that of Fiat; Gold is measured by weight, an intrinsic quality... not by purchasing power. Now, have you any idea of the value of an ounce of Dollars? No such thing. Fiat is only 'measured' by an ephemeral quantity... the number printed on it, the 'face value'.

Bitcoin is farther away from being the numeraire; not only is it simply a number, much as Fiat... but its value is measured in Fiat! Even if Bitcoin becomes internationally accepted as a medium of exchange, and even if it manages to replace the Dollar as the accepted 'numeraire', it can never have an intrinsic measure like Gold has. Gold is unique in being measured by a true, unchanging physical quantity. Gold is unique in storing value for thousands of years. Nothing else in reach of humanity has this unique combination of qualities.

In conclusion, while Bitcoin has some advantages over Fiat, namely anonymity and decentralization, it fails in its claim to being money. Its advantages are also questionable; the intent is to limit the 'mining' of Bitcoins to 26,000,000 units; that is, the 'mining' algorithm gets harder and harder to solve, then impossible after the 26 million Bitcoins are mined. Unfortunately, this announcement could very well be the death knell of Bitcoin; already, some central banks have announced that Bitcoins may become a 'reservable' currency.

Wow, sounds like a major step for Bitcoin, does it not? After all, the 'big banks' seem to be accepting the true value of the Bitcoin, no? What this actually means is banks recognize that they could trade Fiat for Bitcoins... and to actually buy up the 26 million Bitcoins planned would cost a meagre 26 Billion Fiat Dollars. Twenty six billion Dollars is not even small change to the Fiat printers; it is about a week's worth of printing by the US Fed alone. And, once the Bitcoins bought up and locked up in the Fed's 'wallet'... what useful purpose could they serve?

There would be no Bitcoins left in circulation; a perfect corner. If there are no Bitcoins in circulation, how on Earth could they be used as a medium of exchange? And, what could the issuers of Bitcoin possibly do to defend against such a fate? Change the algorithm and increase the 26 million to... 52 million? To 104 million? Join the Fiat printing parade? But then, by the quantity theory of money, Bitcoin would start to lose value, just as Fiat supposedly loses value through 'over-printing'...

We come to the key issue; why search for a 'new money' when we already have the very best money, Gold? Fear of Gold confiscation? Lack of anonymity from an intrusive government? Brutal taxation? Fiat money legal tender laws? All of the above. The answer is not in a new form of money, but in a new social structure, one without Fiat, without Government spying, without drones and swat teams... without IRS, border guards, TSA thugs... on and on. A world of liberty not tyranny. Once this is accomplished, Gold will resume its ancient and vital role as honest money... and not a moment before.

Rudy J. Fritsch was born in Hungary in 1947, and fled Socialist tyranny during the Hungarian Revolution of 1956. His family had lived through WWII and the consequent Hungarian hyperinflation, thus he has intimate experience with financial destruction.

As an engineer and entrepreneur, he ran a successful family business in Canada for decades, at its peak employing over 100 workers, until economic upheaval destroyed the profitability of North

American manufacturing. Driven out of business, he decided to study economics... to discover the cause of this unhappy circumstance.

Bitcoin and Binary Options Trading

Binary options have been becoming more and more popular in the last 2 years. This type of trading has been desired among new traders as they don't need to actually buy anything, just predict whether the asset will move up or down in specified time frame. Those trades are happening in short time frames (30 sec, 1 min, 5 min) but might be months too. If the trader predicted wrongly, they will obviously lose their money. If the trader was right in his/her prediction, they will receive 80-85% payout, depending on the broker.

Binary options are sometimes referred to as 'all-or-nothing options', 'digital options', or 'fixed return options' (FROs), which are traded on the American Stock Exchange.

Bitcoin (BTC) is a digital currency which is created and held electronically and no one controls it. "Bitcoin is an online payment system invented by Satoshi Nakamoto, who published his invention in 2008, and released it as open-source software in 2009. The system is peer-to-peer; users can transact directly without needing an intermediary.Transactions are verified by network nodes and recorded in a public distributed ledger called the blockchain. The ledger uses its own unit of account, also called bitcoin. The system works without a central repository or single administrator, which has led the US Treasury to categorize it as a decentralized virtual currency. Bitcoin is often called the first cryptocurrency... "

Bitcoin as a currency in binary options trading

Bitcoin is now widely used currency and many trading platforms accept it as a method of payment for their clients' trading deposits. There are many benefits using Bitcoin as a currency. The first benefit is "the fact that the cost of transaction is the lowest among all forms of online payment. This is the very reason why Bitcoin was created in the first place, to lower the cost of online transaction. Since there is no central authority managing Bitcoin, no service fee is paid when receiving or transmitting payment." Another reason for traders to use Bitcoin as a currency is that Bitcoin itself is tradeable and they can earn extra Bitcoins that way.

"By having all the trading transactions denoted in Bitcoin, a trader is able to shield himself from the fluctuation of this crypto currency while at the same time earn more of it through profits earned in trading."

Bitcoin as a commodity in binary options trading

With a recent popularity of Bitcoin and its acceptance as a currency, many binary options platforms started using Bitcoin as one of the currencies to trade. so as an asset. Stockbrokers are seeing the value in trading BTC against flat currencies, mainly versus American Dollar.

Today there are 2 main types of Bitcoin binary options platforms:

First-generation brokers - binary options platforms that allow trading on Bitcoin

Second-generation brokers - platforms that offer both Bitcoin funding and Bitcoin trading

First generation brokers - brokers who offer Bitcoin trading:

Coinut - only Bitcoin options exchange platform; programmed as a robust and distributed on Linux operating system coinut.com

BTClevels - Bitcoin binary options trading platform; with or without registration, hassle free btclevels.com

24 Options - one of the first brokers who started offering BTC as an asset 24option.com

Second-generation brokers - brokers who offer Bitcoin funding and trading:

Traderush binary platform - accepts BTC deposits traderush.com

Nadex trading platform -accepts BTC funding and allows BTC trading; offers limited risk, short-term trading, transparency and full regulated market nadex.com

Satoshi Option trading platform - accepts BTC funding and allows BTC trading; doesn't require account registration neither personal details. Payouts are near instantaneous and the service is accessible from anywhere in the world satoshioption.com

BTCOracle platform - Bitcoin only platform - allows BTC funding and trading offering few wallet options and full transparency btcoracle.com

Bitstamp platform - As above, BTC only platform - allows BTC trading and funding but requires login bitstamp.net

Bitcoin Wisdom - allows trading 3 digital currencies, Bitcoins, Litecoins, Altcoins versus other flat currencies and requires login bitcoinwisdom.com

Beast Option - allows BTC funding and trading of Bitcoins and Litecoins; guarantees fairness in pricing regardless of market fluctuations beastoptions.com

When choosing a Bitcoin broker it is important to check their terms and conditions, paying a particular attention to the information whether their Bitcoin Assets are stored in "Deep Cold Storage". It means that Bitcoins are insured and stored offline, where they are not susceptible to hackers.

Trading binary options can be lucrative but only with the right tools.

Conclusion

Thank you again for downloading this book!

I hope this book was able to help you to UNDERSTAND the functions of BITCOIN

Finally, if you enjoyed this book, then I'd like to ask you for a favor, would you be kind enough to leave a review for this book on Amazon? It'd be greatly appreciated!

Thank you and good luck!

I truly do appreciate it!

Best Wishes,

Lee Maxwell

www.ingramcontent.com/pod-product-compliance
Lightning Source LLC
Chambersburg PA
CBHW070109210526
45170CB00013B/795